How Are Rain, Snow, and Hail Alike?

by Ellen Lawrence

Consultants:

Suzy Gazlay, MA
Recipient, Presidential Award for Excellence in Science Teaching

Kimberly Brenneman, PhD
National Institute for Early Education Research, Rutgers University
New Brunswick, New Jersey

BEARPORT
PUBLISHING

New York, New York

Credits

Cover, © Picsfive/Shutterstock, and © Algecireno/Shutterstock, and © Yoshio Tomii/Superstock, and © Science Faction/Superstock; 3, © exclusive studio/Shutterstock; 4L, © Flirt/Superstock; 4R, © Blend Images/Superstock; 5, © Elzbieta Sekowska/Shutterstock; 6, © Sergieiev/Shutterstock; 7, © holbox/Shutterstock; 8–9, © VVO/Shutterstock; 8R, © Denisenko/Shutterstock; 8B, © Tania Zbrodko/Shutterstock; 10, © irin-k/Shutterstock, and © Rafai Fabrykiewicz/Shutterstock; 11, © smit/Shutterstock; 12, © Wilson Bentley/Wikipedia (public domain); 13, © Sari Oneal/Shutterstock; 14, © smit/Shutterstock; 15, © fotoandrius/Shutterstock; 16, © Condor 36/Shutterstock; 17, © ERZ/Wikipedia (public domain); 18, © Horst Sollinger/Imagebroker/FLPA; 19, © Horst Sollinger/Imagebroker/FLPA; 20T; © Bill Frische/Shutterstock; 20BL, © Wilson Bentley/Wikipedia (public domain); 20BR, © Steve Byland/Shutterstock; 21, © Cultura Limited/Superstock; 22L, © Fotoline/Shutterstock, and © design56/Shutterstock, and © Fotoline/Shutterstock; 23TL, © Shutterstock; 23TC, © Bill Frische/Shutterstock; 23TR, © Aguaviva/Shutterstock; 23BL, © smit/Shutterstock; 23BC, © irin-k/Shutterstock; 23BR, © holbox/Shutterstock.

Publisher: Kenn Goin
Creative Director: Spencer Brinker
Design: Emma Randall
Editor: Mark J. Sachner
Photo Researcher: Ruby Tuesday Books Ltd

Library of Congress Cataloging-in-Publication Data

Lawrence, Ellen, 1967–
 How are rain, snow, and hail alike? / by Ellen Lawrence.
  p. cm. — (Weather wise)
 Includes bibliographical references and index.
 ISBN 978-1-61772-403-9 (library binding) — ISBN 1-61772-403-3 (library binding)
 1. Precipitation (Meteorology)—Juvenile literature. I. Title.
 QC924.7.L39 2012
 551.57'7—dc23
                        2011049582

For more information, write to Bearport Publishing Company, Inc., 45 West 21st Street, Suite 3B, New York, New York 10010. Printed in the United States of America in North Mankato, Minnesota.

10 9 8 7 6 5 4 3 2 1

Contents

Different in Many Ways

When heavy rain falls from the sky, it quickly makes people wet.

When soft snow falls, it gently settles on skin and clothes.

When icy hail falls, it can hurt anyone it hits!

Raindrops, snowflakes, and **hailstones** are different from each other in many ways.

Are there also ways they are alike?

snow

rain

Hailstones are small balls of ice that fall from clouds. Usually, they are no bigger than a pea. In 2010, however, a giant hailstone measuring eight inches (20.3 cm) across fell in South Dakota!

hailstones

It All Begins with Water

One way in which rain, snow, and hail are alike is that they all fall from the sky.

How does this happen?

It all begins with the water in oceans, rivers, lakes, and ponds.

As the sun warms the water some of it changes.

It turns from a **liquid** into a **gas** called **water vapor**.

The vapor floats up into the air.

Pour some water onto the sidewalk on a warm, sunny day. Watch what happens to the water. It looks like it's disappearing, but it isn't! The water is changing into invisible water vapor.

Water vapor floats up into the air.

It's not possible to see water vapor. Yet it is in the air all around us. Every second of every day, some of Earth's water is changing into vapor.

Making Clouds

The water vapor soon rises high above Earth, where the air is cold.

The cold air causes the vapor to turn into tiny water droplets that stick to bits of dust floating in the air.

These droplets join with billions of others to form clouds!

clouds

Take a soda can from the refrigerator. After a few minutes, you will see drops of water on the outside of the can. How did this happen? The water vapor in the air touched the cold can and changed back into liquid water!

Water can change from a liquid into a gas and then back to a liquid again!

clouds

9

Making Rain

Inside a cloud, the tiny water droplets join together to make bigger drops.

Soon, the drops get even bigger and heavier.

Then they fall back to Earth as raindrops.

The raindrops are water that has moved from Earth, into the sky, and back to Earth again.

This movement of water is called the **water cycle**.

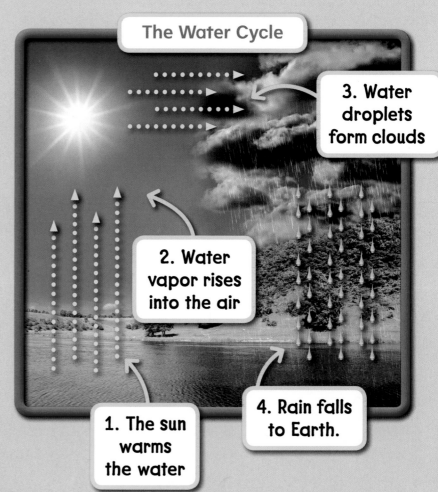

The Water Cycle

3. Water droplets form clouds

2. Water vapor rises into the air

1. The sun warms the water

4. Rain falls to Earth.

Rain falls into oceans, lakes, rivers, and ponds. It might even make a puddle on land. Soon, the rainwater may begin to turn into vapor and go through the water cycle again.

Rain forms inside clouds and then falls to Earth. Snow falls from the sky, too. How do you think snow forms?

Let It Snow!

Sometimes the air around a cloud is very cold.

Then the water droplets freeze into tiny ice crystals instead of becoming raindrops.

The crystals are the size of the period at the end of this sentence.

They stick together to form snowflakes.

Then snow falls from the cloud instead of rain.

snowflakes

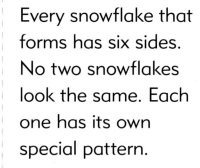

Every snowflake that forms has six sides. No two snowflakes look the same. Each one has its own special pattern.

Snow stays on the ground when the air is cold. When the air warms up, what do you think happens to it?

13

A Disappearing Snowman
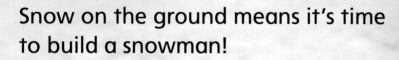

Snow on the ground means it's time to build a snowman!

When the weather stays very cold, a snowman may last for weeks.

When the air warms up, however, the snowman begins to melt.

The warmth of the sun soon changes the snowman back into water.

Water can change from a liquid to **solid** ice and back to a liquid again.

water from melted snow

How Do Hailstones Form?

Hailstones form inside a thunderstorm cloud when the wind blows the cloud's tiny water droplets way up high.

There, the air is super cold and the droplets freeze into balls of ice.

These frozen ice balls, called hailstones, fall back down lower in the cloud.

More water droplets stick to them.

Then, the hailstones get blown high up in the cloud again and the new droplets freeze.

thunderstorm cloud

Look at the icy hailstones in this picture. What do you think will happen to them if they get warm?

(See answer on p. 24.)

Different, but Alike

Raindrops, snowflakes, and hailstones may look very different from each other.

Yet there are many ways in which they are alike.

They all develop high in the sky inside clouds.

Then they fall to Earth.

Most important of all, they are all made of water!

hailstones

snowflakes

The different forms that water takes when it falls from a cloud are called precipitation. Rain, snow, and hail are all types of precipitation.

raindrops

Science Lab

Rain, Snow, and Hail Notebook

In a notebook, keep track of the precipitation that falls where you live. Use the chart at right as a guide to record your measurements.

How to Measure . . .

Rain: Leave a clear glass jar outside. Whenever it rains, use a ruler to measure how much water fell into the jar.

Snow: Use a ruler to measure the snow's depth in a place where the ground is flat.

Hail: Use a ruler to measure the width of one hailstone.

hailstones

Precipitation Record

Date	Precipitation	Measurement
Nov 21	🌧	1 inch (2.5 cm)
Nov 23	🌧	half an inch (1.3 cm)
Nov 30	⚪⚪	half an inch wide (1.3 cm)
Dec 3	🌧	half an inch (1.3 cm)
Dec 10	❄	2 inches (5 cm)

Science Words

gas (GASS) matter that floats in air and is neither a liquid or a solid; most gases, such as water vapor, are invisible

hailstones (HAYL-stohnz) small balls of ice formed in storm clouds from frozen water droplets

liquid (LIK-wid) something that flows and changes its shape to fit whatever container it is placed in

solid (SOL-id) having a definite size and shape; the state of water when it becomes ice

water cycle (WAW-tur SYE-kuhl) the movement of water from Earth, up into the sky to form clouds, and back down to Earth again

water vapor (WAW-tur VAY-pur) water that has changed into a gas; water vapor rises and spreads out through the air

Index

Read More

Burby, Liza N. *Hail (Extreme Weather)*. New York: PowerKids Press (2003).

Cassino, Mark, with Jon Nelson. *The Story of Snow: The Science of Winter's Wonder*. San Francisco: Chronicle Books (2009).

Purslow, Frances. *Precipitation (Science Matters)*. New York: Weigl (2006).

Learn More Online

To learn more about rain, snow, and hail, visit
www.bearportpublishing.com/WeatherWise

Answer

page 19: They will melt.

About the Author

Ellen Lawrence lives in the United Kingdom. Her favorite books to write are those about animals and nature. In fact, the first book Ellen bought for herself, when she was six years old, was the story of a gorilla named Patty Cake that was born in New York's Central Park Zoo.